*The*

# BREATH

*of Life*

*The*
# BREATH
*of Life*

## A Simple Way to Pray

✳

Ron DelBene
with Herb & Mary Montgomery

UPPER
ROOM BOOKS
NASHVILLE

THE BREATH OF LIFE
Revised Edition

Cover Design by Bruce Gore
Cover Photograph by Westlight/ © Chuck O'Rear
First Printing: October 1992 (7)
Library of Congress Catalog Number: 91-65724
ISBN: 0-8358-0647-2

Printed in the United States of America

*To all those*
*who have shared their lives*
*with me in prayer*

# Also by the Authors

*Christmas Remembered*
*From the Heart*

## The Into the Light Collection
*Into the Light*
*When I'm Alone*
*Near Life's End*
*A Time to Mourn (also on cassette)*
*Study Guide*

## The Times of Change, Times of Challenge Series
*When You Are Getting Married*
*When Your Child Is Baptized*
*When You Are Facing Surgery*
*When an Aging Loved One Needs Care*
*When You Are Facing a Decision*
*When You Are Living with an Illness That Is Not Your Own*

## The Breath of Life Series:
*The Breath of Life*
*The Hunger of the Heart*
*Alone with God*

# C O N T E N T S

# P R E F A C E

$M$y friendship with Ron DelBene has established itself through the years. We first met when Ron had a newly acquired master's degree in theology, and we both worked at a publishing company in Minneapolis—Ron as their national consultant in religion and me as an editor. Although our careers have long since taken different paths, we have remained friends, and I have had the privilege of watching Ron grow personally and professionally.

Ron came of age during the turbulent sixties when religious institutions and traditional values were being challenged. He met those challenges with enthusiasm and a willingness to learn and grow—traits that have characterized his ministry and his own spiritual journey. Always moving on, Ron brought a dynamic force and his personal style to teaching, campus ministry, and renewal movements. After experiencing success in the business world, he was called to be ordained a priest in 1979 and in the years since has been active in parish ministry. Spiritual direction has long been an important part of Ron's call to serve. In addition to giving spiritual direction privately, he has traveled extensively to conduct conferences and lead retreats on spiritual development. In all his endeavors, Ron has been nurtured and supported by his family that includes Eleanor, his wife, and their children, Paul and Anne.

The sum of Ron's experiences gives him a particular empathy with those searching for meaning and purpose in their lives. A person of prayer himself, Ron feels strongly that prayer is at the heart of life. At seminars and retreats and in private sessions on spiritual direction, he has helped people discover their breath prayer—a prayer so simple that, when it is practiced faithfully, it comes as easily and naturally as breathing.

When Ron told me about the breath prayer and its effect on people's lives, I encouraged him to extend his ministry by writing about it. He always found reasons not to, and finding time invariably headed the list. Finally, I suggested that we collaborate, and the result was *The Breath of Life: A Simple Way to Pray*. After its publication, we collaborated on two other books: *The Hunger of the Heart: A Call to Spiritual Growth* and *Alone with God: A Guide for Personal Retreats*. Some ten years later all three books were still much in demand but needed updating. Ron and I invited my wife, Mary, who is also a writer, to join us in revising the books that are being reissued as The Breath of Life Series. The three of us want to thank Janice Lilly for reading the books and making editorial suggestions.

Ron encourages those who come to him for spiritual direction to record their thoughts in journals that they then share with him. These deeply felt writings let us glimpse what happens when we choose to let God enter more fully into our lives. A number of journal entries are included in this book, and all are used with permission. The entries appear as they were written, but in the interest of privacy, names and some identifying details have been changed. The hope of those who let their entries be used is that others will benefit from their experiences.

Throughout *The Breath of Life* you will find numerous quotations about prayer and the spiritual life. For the most part they were written during earlier centuries when the male pronoun referred to both male and female and was used exclusively in referring to God. Ron chose the quotations because he believes that what the writers have to say is of such value that readers will not let the noninclusive language get in the way of the message.

*The Breath of Life* is an invitation to broaden your spiritual horizons by discovering your breath prayer—a prayer that will put on your lips what is always in your heart. The hope of all of us who have worked on this book is that you will discover for yourself how this short, simple prayer of praise and petition can help you more fully experience the presence and power of God in your everyday life.

HERB MONTGOMERY

# When God's Time and Our Time Intersect

Often things happen to us that have a meaning we don't understand at the time. Yet we *know* that something of unusual importance has occurred. We may be sitting with a friend or reading or listening to music or walking alone in nature when something alerts us. Like Moses at the burning bush, we proceed carefully, aware that we are on holy ground. God's time and our time intersect, and we have the gift to know it.

These experiences are not as rare as some would have us think. Based on my own life and what others have shared with me, I have come to believe that being aware of when God's time and our time intersect is not only a possibility—it is something we are called to. My own life has included a number of such experiences. As I share a few of them, you may feel that some, or all of them, are quite ordinary. Indeed, they may be, but while each was occurring I was aware of myself and my God in a mysterious and beautiful way.

I was an adult before I could share how, as a young boy, I knelt in a candle-lit mission church in a small Ohio city and knew that I had seen into heaven, but dared not say so to anyone. God's time and my time had intersected, and as a child, I had the gift to know it.

Another incident occurred one Sunday evening in October of 1963. The weekend retreat I had attended was over, and those of us who participated were visiting in the church basement. It had been a powerful weekend, and I sensed that all of us were feeling especially close to God. I happened to be standing next to an elderly street person who had been brought to the retreat by the retreat leader. The leader's ministry included working with inmates at the county jail, and when he was giving a retreat, he would request that certain regulars at the jail be released to his custody. I began talking with the elderly gentleman from the jail, and at one point tears filmed his eyes. With great emotion in his voice, he said, "Why, *oh why*, did it take so long for me to have this experience with God?"

Out of the core of my being, and matching his intensity of emotion, I said, "And why has it happened to me so *early*? When I'm so *young*?" In that moment I had a flash of awareness that my journey was lifelong and that I had been called to be attentive for all my days. God's time and my time had again intersected.

Yet another incident occurred when I was a graduate student studying theology and having a difficult time reconciling my textbook learning with all the social justice activity of the mid-sixties. In trying to decide whether to cut back on my classes and become more involved in social justice ministry, I went to talk to one of my professors. He was someone in whom I had great confidence and with whom I had previously shared what was happening in my life. At one point in our conversation there was a silence and he said, "Let's pray the Lord's Prayer together." As I said the words, *Our*

*Father,* I began to weep, and the pieces of all the issues I had been dealing with began to flow together. God's power was present. *And I knew it.*

Again, on my wedding day, I felt God's presence in a special way. As I was waiting to go down the aisle, I glanced off to the right. There was Eleanor coming through an archway, the whole of which shone with light. The overwhelming presence of beauty that I sensed at that moment has remained throughout the many years of our marriage.

A common thread runs through these experiences. In each of them my heart was touched, opened, and examined. At those times I *knew* what the psalmist meant by "Yahweh, you examine me and know me" (Psalm 139:1, JB).

As I have traveled my own journey of the spirit, and as others have shared their journeys with me, I have come to believe that *we all have the gift of knowing when God's time and our time intersect.* After I had made this point at a conference, a young man came up afterward and said, "I want to know more about this gift of knowing. What do you base it on? Is there some foundation?"

"What I believe," I told him, "is that God is present to us and we are in God's presence in every action of our lives. Becoming aware of this is spiritual growth, and living as attentively as possible in that reality is what life is all about."

There are many approaches to living in God's presence, and in this book I share mine. To begin, I ask that you look at your own life.

• Have you had an experience that awakened your inner spirit?

• Did you feel that you were in some way on holy ground?

• Were you so touched by the experience that you tucked it away in your heart, not sharing it with anyone?

If the life of the Spirit is new to you, or if prayer is new to you, or if for any other reason you feel that your time and God's time have not intersected, be patient. Together in this book we are companions on the way— companions on a journey that takes us deeper into the life of the Spirit. On this journey you will discover a simple way to pray that will help you feel God's presence, not just in extraordinary occurrences but in the ordinariness of everyday life.

*The day of my spiritual*
*awakening*
*was the day I saw*
*and knew I saw*
*all things in God*
*and God*
*in all things.*

✳

Mechtild of Magdeburg (c. 1209–c.1283)
German mystical writer
From *Meditations with Mechtild of Magdeburg*

*God, you are my God, I am seeking you,*
*my soul is thirsting for you,*
*my flesh is longing for you,*
*a land parched, weary and waterless;*
*I long to gaze on you in the Sanctuary,*
*and to see your power and glory.*

*Your love is better than life itself,*
*my lips will recite your praise;*
*all my life I will bless you,*
*in your name lift up my hands.*

✳

Psalm 63:1-4, JB

# CHAPTER 2

## *Called to Be Prayerful*

Most of us who come from a Christian background have learned to say prayers, read prayers, listen to prayers, memorize prayers. We speak of mental prayers, of prayerful meditation, of reciting prayers, of studying prayers. But how often are we challenged to *become* prayer? How often are we called to be so God-centered that we become other-centered and think of prayer as a gift of ourselves to another person?

The gift of ourselves varies with the circumstances. In one situation, the gift might be a listening ear or a helping hand, and in another, a warm embrace, a bit of our time, a word of encouragement or comfort or cheer. The gift of ourselves is almost certain to involve us in social justice issues—in clothing the naked, feeding the hungry, giving drink to the thirsty, finding shelter for the homeless. This is the other-centeredness the apostle Paul refers to when he writes, "it is no longer I who live, but it is Christ who lives in me" (Gal. 2:20).

So far you may feel that you fall far short of the ideal Paul speaks of. This is not cause for discouragement. Few of us when looking in a mirror see a saint reflected back. We are all at different places on our spiritual journey, but wherever we are, taking even a small step forward makes the goal less distant. When we focus on the present—on where we live and love and interact with others—opportunities to become prayer are all around us.

Prayer involves us in seeking, growing, loving. But in our desire to draw closer to God, there is a danger that we will wear ourselves out with a multitude of prayers that can easily become routine or even meaningless. When prayer comes not from the mind alone but is integrated into our whole being, we become more aware of what prayer can do for us and for our relationship with God.

A truly prayerful person lives more and more in an attitude of prayer—more and more turned toward God. Such a person is not constantly beseeching God, but is instead attentive to the life of the Spirit and able to hear: "Be still, and know that I am God" (Psalm 46:10). Through attentive stillness, we are better able to concentrate on where we are on our spiritual journey and where God is calling us.

Scripture tells us, "Be perfect, therefore, as your heavenly Father is perfect" (Matt. 5:48). *Be perfect as God is perfect! Isn't that asking just too much?* Indeed, it is. Expecting perfection from ourselves and others leads to problems too numerous to pursue here. We can avoid many of these problems by understanding that the intent of the passage lies in knowing the derivation of the word *perfect* and its meaning in the scriptural context. *Perfect* means "whole" or "integrated" or "together." God is not calling us to be perfect in the commonly understood use of the word, but rather to be whole, fully-integrated people with body, mind, and spirit in harmony. When we are functioning as a whole, we are in communion with life; we are able to see, hear, and respond with a full and joyous heart.

Prayer is a search for meaning, and through prayer we try to discover God's will for our lives. Many people view God's will as something chipped in stone at the time of their birth. They then spend a lifetime trying to determine what it is God has in mind for them. Much of the frustration of this quest is eliminated if we understand what is meant by God's will.

The word *will*, which we translate from the Latin *voluntas*, means "yearning" in both Hebrew and Greek. So the question "What is God's will for me?" is more precisely "What is God's yearning for me?" Yearning describes the longing that two people in love have for one another: not a yearning of the mind alone or of the heart alone, but of the *whole being*. When someone yearns for us, our yearning is awakened, which in turn intensifies the yearning of the other until we come together in some way. Thus God's yearning is not something we find outside ourselves, but rather something we become aware of and experience from within. In trying to determine whether our yearning is a response to God's yearning for us, we might ask ourselves these questions:

- Will following my yearning make me more loving?
- Will I be a better servant of my gifts?
- Will I feel more fulfilled?
- Will I have a greater sense of inner peace?

When we can answer yes to these questions, we know that our yearning and God's yearning for us are one and the same.

The breath prayer—which Chapter 5 will lead you to discover—keeps us attentive to God. This attentiveness leads to a greater sense of God's presence in our lives and of where we are being called. We are then no longer simply prayerful people, but we are on our way to becoming prayer.

## Crucible of Prayer

*It seems clear to me
that in some way we must unite
our wills with God's will.*

*But it is in the effects and
deeds following afterwards
that one discerns the true
value of prayer.*

*There is no better crucible for
testing prayer than compassion.*

Teresa of Avila (1515–1582)
From *Meditations with Teresa of Avila*

*Thoughts continue to jostle in your head like mosquitoes. To stop this jostling, you must bind the mind with one thought, or the thought of One only. An aid to this is a short prayer, which helps the mind to become simple and united. . . . Together with the short prayer, you must keep your thought and attention turned towards God. But if you limit your prayer to words only, you are as "sounding brass."*

Theophan the Recluse,
nineteenth-century monk, bishop,
and spiritual director
From *The Art of Prayer: An Orthodox Anthology*

# CHAPTER 3

# The Scriptural Base for Unceasing Prayer

For prayerful people, scripture is the living word that provides signposts along the path of their spiritual journey. The call to be people of prayer is woven through both the Hebrew and Christian scriptures. In this passage from the Hebrew scripture, Moses beseeches the people of Israel never to forget the deeds of Yahweh, and to make this remembrance part of their daily lives:

> Listen, Israel: Yahweh our God is the one Yahweh. You shall love Yahweh your God with all your heart, with all your soul, with all your strength. Let these words I urge on you today be written on your heart. You shall repeat them to your children and say them over to them whether at rest in your house or walking abroad, at your lying down or at your rising; you shall fasten them on your hand as a sign and on your forehead as a circlet; you shall write them on the doorposts of your house and on your gates.
>
> Deuteronomy 6:4-9, JB

Like our faith ancestors we, too, need reminders of God's action in our lives. The letters of the Christian scripture admonish us to keep ourselves mindful of God through unceasing prayer. In the letter to the Hebrews (13:15-16) we read:

> Through him, then, let us continually offer a sacrifice of praise to God, that is, the fruit of lips that confess his name. Do not neglect to do good and to share what you have, for such sacrifices are pleasing to God.

To the Thessalonians (1 Thess. 5:16-18), the apostle Paul wrote: "Rejoice always, pray without ceasing, give thanks in all circumstances."

In Colossians 4:2, we are told: "Devote yourselves to prayer, keeping alert in it with thanksgiving."

No matter what the circumstances of our lives, we are called to respond with prayer. Romans 12:12 counsels: "Rejoice in hope, be patient in suffering, persevere in prayer."

In Ephesians 6:18, we are told: "Pray in the Spirit at all times in every prayer and supplication."

To pray without ceasing on every possible occasion means that *we are to be in a state of remembrance of what God has done, and is doing, for us.* We are to praise God and to ask for what we need. When we do this, our prayer is one of praise and petition.

In addition, we are told to pray in the Spirit, which is understood more fully by examining the Hebrew word *ruach*. It is a word that can be translated as "wind," "breath," or "spirit." The spirit, or *ruach* of God, is breathed into all living beings.

Time and again throughout scripture, we see God breathing life into creation. In Ezekiel 37:9, we read:

> Then he said to me, "Prophesy to the breath, prophesy, mortal, and say to the breath: Thus says the Lord God: Come from the four winds, O breath, and breathe upon these slain, that they may live."

Likewise in John 20:22, we find reference to the Spirit being breathed upon the disciples: "When he had said this, he breathed on them and said to them, 'Receive the Holy Spirit.' "

Genesis 1:1 speaks of God's Spirit being imparted in the wind:

> In the beginning when God created the heavens and the earth, the earth was a formless void and darkness covered the face of the deep, while a wind from God swept over the face of the waters.

In John 3:8, we again see God's Spirit as wind: "The wind blows where it chooses, and you hear the sound of it, but you do not know where it comes from or where it goes. So it is with everyone who is born of the Spirit."

The scriptures also speak of God's Spirit entering into us. In the Hebrew scriptures, the prophet Ezekiel (36:27) says: "I will put my spirit within you, and make you follow my statutes and be careful to observe my ordinances."

Paul, in a letter to the Galatians (4:6) writes: "And because you are children, God has sent the Spirit of his Son into our hearts, crying, "Abba! Father!"

Through prayer we feel a oneness with God. When we cannot pray for ourselves, the Spirit speaks for us:

Likewise the Spirit helps us in our weakness; for we do not know how to pray as we ought, but that very Spirit intercedes with sighs too deep for words. And God, who searches the heart, knows what is in the mind of the Spirit, because the Spirit intercedes for the saints according to the will of God.

Romans 8:26-27

What a comfort to know that the Spirit intercedes for us in times when we are too filled with doubt or sorrow or anger to reach out to God on our own. But aside from those times, how do we take responsibility for our prayer lives? How do we remain constant in prayer? When our schedules are already overcrowded, how can we possibly praise and thank God unceasingly? An answer lies in the breath prayer—a prayer that helps us pray without ceasing and keeps us mindful that we share the breath of God.

*Thus ceaseless prayer keeps our mental air free from the dark clouds and winds of the spirits of evil. And when the air of the heart is pure, there is nothing to prevent the Divine light of Jesus shining in. . . .*

❋

Hesychius,
an early fifth-century preacher and
teacher of the church in Palestine,
known for his knowledge of scripture.
From his writings to his friend
Theodulus

From *Writings from the Philokalia on Prayer of
the Heart*

This is why I bless God in my heart
without ceasing
for every earthly thing.

And this is why God gave us a mouth—
to praise God
with inconceivable praise
in common with all creatures
with all our doings
at all times.

✳

Mechtild of Magdeburg (c. 1209–c.1283)
German mystical writer
From *Meditations with Mechtild of Magdeburg*

# What Is the Breath Prayer?

The breath prayer is a short prayer of praise and petition that has been used since ancient times. As we breathe unceasingly, our breathing supports life and renews our corporeal system. When we use the breath prayer to develop our ability to pray unceasingly, God's love supports and renews us.

Historically, the breath prayer rose out of the Psalms. Repeated phrases from the Psalms became short prayers to remind one of the entire psalm.

In some religious traditions, various forms of a breath prayer have been called "aspiratory" or "ejaculatory" prayers. The term *aspiratory* comes from the Latin word meaning "to breathe," and *ejaculatory* from the sport of javelin throwing. Such prayers have traditionally been short and have risen from individual circumstances. In times of stress, need, or joy we may pray, "Jesus, help me" or "O God, hear my prayer" or "Praise to thee, O God." Such prayers rise spontaneously from within, sometimes flowing from us without our being consciously aware that we are praying.

It is said that Ignatius of Antioch, who was killed early in the second century because of his faith in Jesus, used a short prayer over and over while in prison. When questioned by his jailers, who thought his words were some kind of incantation, Ignatius explained that his teacher (believed to be John the Apostle) had taught him to have on his lips what was always in his heart.

Having on our lips what is always in our heart is the essence of the breath prayer, the roots of which go deep in our spiritual heritage. Within the Christian tradition of the East there is a breath prayer called the Jesus Prayer: "Lord Jesus Christ, Son of God, have mercy on me, a sinner." The prayer grew out of a need to create a disciplined form of prayer for the thousands of monks and others who were seeking a deeper relationship with God. The Jesus Prayer served as a touchstone, compressing into a very few words all the doctrine one needed to believe in order to be saved.

The Jesus Prayer was formulated in the sixth century and enjoyed a revival in the Christian church of the East, most notably in Greece and Russia, in the fourteenth and nineteenth centuries. *The Way of a Pilgrim,* a classic book on spirituality by an anonymous nineteenth-century peasant, describes the beauty and use of this breath prayer. Intent upon a deeper spirituality, the devout peasant visits an esteemed elder who quotes to him from sacred writings:

> If, in spite of all effort, you cannot enter the interior of the heart in the way which was explained to you, then do what I will tell you and with God's help you will reach your goal. . . . While fighting distractions, diligently and continuously say, "Lord Jesus Christ, have mercy on me!" If you will persevere for some time then, without any doubt, the path to the heart will be opened to you. This has been verified through experience.

After following the elder's suggestion for some time, the pilgrim wrote:

> Then I went to see the elder and told him everything in detail. He listened to me and then said, "Praise be to God that now you have both a longing for the Prayer and that the recitation of it comes easily. . . . Call on the name of Jesus all your waking moments, without counting, and humbly resign yourself to God's will expecting help from Him. I believe that He will direct your path and will not forsake you."
>
> After receiving this direction, I spent the rest of the summer reciting the name of Jesus vocally and I enjoyed great peace. During my sleep I often dreamed that I was praying. And if I happened to meet people during the day they all seemed as close to me as if they were my kinsmen, even though I did not know them. My thoughts had quieted down completely; I thought only of the Prayer, to which my mind now began to listen, and my heart produced certain warmth and gladness.

In recent years the Jesus Prayer has again become a way of prayer for many people. Some use the traditional prayer shortened to "Lord Jesus, Son of God, have mercy on me." Others prefer, "Lord Jesus Christ, have mercy," or even the brief, "Jesus, mercy."

Back when I was a college freshman I knew nothing of this way of praying, but in my deeply-felt desire to draw closer to God, I discovered it on my own. After studying for college exams one cold December night, I decided to take a walk before going to bed. I can still recall the frostiness of the air, the sprinkling of stars in the black sky, the crunch of snow under my boots. As I walked along the nearly-deserted streets of Erie, Pennsylvania, my thoughts turned to my inner spirit. I felt restless and unfulfilled. What was I seeking? Where was I going with my spiritual life?

That night I made two significant decisions: I consciously decided that I was called to be on a journey with my God and that, as a foundation of my faith life, I would use a short prayer to keep me spiritually disciplined.

In the ensuing months I made it a point to pray often. When I was going for a walk, driving, or waiting in line, I said my short prayer. In much the same way that I was breathing without consciously thinking about it, prayer was going on spontaneously within my being.

Only later did I learn that I had discovered a way to pray that had been used through the centuries. But instead of using the Jesus Prayer, or one of its variations, I realized that a more personal prayer had come to me. It arose from my personal need and clarified who I was. I felt then, and continue to believe, that the better we understand ourselves and our needs, the better we are able to understand our relationship with God.

Since that long-ago winter night, I have instructed countless people in this personal approach to prayer. The goal has always been to help them arrive at a breath prayer that is distinctly their own—a prayer that puts on their lips what is deep in their heart. Just as breathing goes on naturally within our bodies, our personal prayer of praise and petition plays in our mind and sings in our heart even when we are not focusing on it. As we find more and more ways to use our prayer, we are sustained and renewed by the sense that we are in God's presence. I invite you to experience the many gifts and insights that come from using the breath prayer, a prayer we discover for ourselves.

*Sisters and brothers, listen.*
*Make your heart crystal clear within.*
*Your senses will be opened*
*and your soul so transparent*
*that we will see*
*into*
*the wisdom*
*of God.*

✳

Mechtild of Magdeburg (c. 1209–c.1283)
German mystical writer
From *Meditations with Mechtild of Magdeburg*

When we come to any new form of prayer, it is helpful to learn from someone who has used the form for a long time. Even though we might not think we have a prayer within us, we do.

There is an often repeated story about a gentle monk who was well known for his prayer life. Someone younger came to him and asked how he had reached the point where prayer was constant.

"Looking back," said the monk, "it seems that the prayer has always been deep in my heart. Once it was like an underground spring covered over with a stone. Then one day Jesus came along and removed the stone. The spring has been bubbling ever since."

✳

# Discovering Your Breath Prayer

The breath prayer lies within us like a tiny seed that, when nurtured, grows and flowers, providing a new and deeper awareness of God's presence. To discover your breath prayer, follow these five easy steps:

### Step One

Sit in a comfortable position. Close your eyes, and remind yourself that God loves you and that you are in God's loving presence. Recall a passage from scripture that puts you in a prayerful frame of mind. Consider "The Lord is my Shepherd" (Psalm 23:1) or "Be still, and know that I am God!" (Psalm 46:10).

### Step Two

With your eyes closed, imagine that God is calling you by name. Hear God asking: "(*Your name*), what do you want?"

### Step Three

Answer God with whatever comes directly from your heart. Your answer might be a single word, such as *peace* or *love* or *forgiveness*. Your answer could instead be a phrase or brief sentence, such as "I want to feel your forgiveness," or "I want to know your love."

Because the prayer is personal, it naturally rises out of our present concerns. One person may focus on physical health, another on becoming still and peaceful within, still another on learning to hear God's voice more clearly or being released from guilt. Your response to God's question "What do you want?" becomes the heart of your prayer.

### Step Four

Choose your favorite name for God. Choices commonly made include God, Jesus, Creator, Teacher, Light, Lord, Spirit, Shepherd.

### Step Five

Combine your name for God with your answer to God's question "What do you want?" You then have your prayer. For example:

| What I Want | Name I Call God | Possible Prayer |
| --- | --- | --- |
| peace | God | Let me know your peace, O God. |
| love | Jesus | Jesus, let me feel your love. |
| rest | Shepherd | My Shepherd, let me rest in thee. |
| guidance | Eternal Light | Eternal Light, guide me in your way. |

What do you do if several ideas occur? Write down the various possibilities and then eliminate and/or combine ideas until you have focused your prayer. You may want many things, but it is possible to narrow wants down to specific needs basic to your well-being. Thus the question to ask yourself is *What do I want that will make me feel most whole?* As you achieve a greater feeling of wholeness, serenity will flow into the many areas of your life.

When you have gotten at the heart of your needs, search for words that give them expression. Then work with the words until you have a prayer of six or eight syllables that flows smoothly when spoken aloud or expressed as a heart thought. A prayer of six or eight syllables has a natural rhythm. Anything longer or shorter usually does not flow easily when said repeatedly.

Some prayers are more rhythmic when God's name is placed at the beginning; other prayers flow better with it at the end. Sometimes all that is needed to give the prayer rhythm is changing the words around. For instance, "God, let me know your peace" may be more rhythmic for you by changing it to "Let me know your peace, O God." When your prayer seems right for you, use it again and again throughout the day. (Ideas for incorporating the prayer into your life are found in Chapter 7.)

Whatever your prayer, it needs to be *your own.* Several years ago at a conference some of the people chose to share their breath prayers with one another. I heard such prayers as "Jesus lead my son to you" and "Bless my family, Lord." While these are fine prayers, they are not what the breath prayer is about.

When Jesus said to the blind man, "What do you want?" the man did not say, "Lord, that I may see so that I can make a living and support others." No, the question drew from the blind man his deepest yearning—the yearning that would make him feel most whole—and he said, "Lord, that I may see." Likewise, when you hear Jesus say, "What do you want?" even though you may feel you are being selfish, you are to get at the true desire of *your* heart and respond with whatever expresses *your* deepest need. That, then, becomes your breath prayer—a prayer that gives you a way to begin to pray unceasingly and feel the nearness of God.

*Let no one think, my fellow Christians, that only priests and monks need to pray without ceasing, and not lay[people]. No, no: every Christian without exception ought to dwell always in prayer . . . the Name of God must be remembered in prayer as often as one draws breath.*

✳

Attributed to Gregory Palamas,
a 14th-century mystical writer on
prayer
From *The Art of Prayer: An Orthodox
Anthology*

## The Call

*The Lord desires intensely that we*
*love him*
*and seek his company.*
*So much so that*
*from time to time*
*he calls us to draw near to him.*

*The call comes through words spoken by*
*other good people,*
*or through sermons,*
*or through what is read in books,*
*or through the many things that are*
*heard and by which God calls,*
*or by illnesses and trials,*
*or in enjoying the beauty of creation,*
*or also through a truth that he teaches*
*during the brief moments*
*we spend in prayer.*

Teresa of Avila (1515-1582)
From *Meditations with Teresa of Avila*

# Questions about the Breath Prayer

When I introduce the breath prayer at a conference or seminar on spiritual growth, questions usually follow. I always feel gratified by this because it lets me know that the people in the audience are serious and discerning— not willing to take up a spiritual discipline unless they feel comfortable with its merit and its rightness for them. Following are some typically asked questions and my responses to them.

*Is it possible that I am already using a breath prayer?*
After I have taught the breath prayer, people frequently tell me that they have been using such a prayer without calling it that. What I usually discover, however, is that these people do not stay with a *specific* prayer for very long. Instead they tend to alternate their prayers or have crisis prayers they fall back on whenever a serious problem arises. I encourage those who have used a number of such prayers to go back through the process and discover their most *basic* response to God's question: "(Your name), what do you want?" Then I urge them to stay with that prayer. Staying with a single prayer that expresses our deepest need is a helpful way to focus on God's power and love.

*Once I begin using the breath prayer, what happens to other prayers I have been saying?*

The breath prayer is not intended to replace prayers you have been saying, or your ways of expressing them. I liken prayer life to a house that includes many parts, all of which require a foundation. Think of the place where you live. Each room serves a purpose. While cooking in the kitchen, sleeping in the bedroom, or gathering with friends in the living area, you give little thought to the supporting foundation—unless, of course, it is faulty! Normally we assume the foundation is solid, doing what it is intended to do. The breath prayer can serve as the foundation upon which you build your life of prayer.

Immediately after discovering your breath prayer you might find it so new and exciting that it is more like an addition to your prayer life than a foundation. But as you become accustomed to using your prayer, the newness will be tempered, and the prayer's value as the foundation of your spiritual life will become apparent. If you are beginning your prayer life with the breath prayer, regard it as the foundation upon which to build in the future.

All forms of prayer bring us more and more into an awareness of being in God's presence. Reading scripture, being faithful to morning and evening prayers, saying intercessory prayers, attending communal worship services—all are important spiritual disciplines. But each of these activities has a beginning and ending point, whereas the breath prayer is not limited to fixed times. Because it can be said anywhere at anytime, it becomes the link that holds all our activities together. Many people also find the breath prayer helpful in calming themselves so that they can give greater attention to other prayer forms. Two or three minutes of saying the breath prayer usually provides the desired sense of peace.

*Why is the breath prayer so short?*

The prayer is short because it flows from a basic need that can be expressed in a few words. Also, the brevity of the prayer makes it easy to remember and thereby suitable for people of all ages in all kinds of circumstances. Most of us find that our breath prayer takes on a sing-song quality, and no matter what we are doing, the words that speak of our deepest need play in our mind and sing in our heart throughout the day.

*How is the breath prayer different from the mantra used in non-Christian forms of meditation?*

People who are given a mantra in such practices as transcendental meditation are usually given it as part of a mystical ritual or ceremony and cautioned to limit its use. Typically those practicing this form of meditation focus on their mantra twice a day for twenty minutes.

There is nothing magical or mysterious about the breath prayer. It is not a chant or word or sound given to us by someone else. Nor does it involve secret ceremonies or rituals. Instead, it is a self-discovered prayer that arises within each of us as our personal response to God. Best of all, the breath prayer can be used anywhere at any time. Many of us find it to be the first step toward praying unceasingly.

*Is the breath prayer vain repetition?*

Whenever I am asked this question, I assume the person asking has in mind the passage from Matthew 6:7 in which Jesus warns against insincere prayer and the mistaken belief that we will be heard for our "many words." Certainly prayer can be said with only the lips, but the personal nature of the breath prayer makes it unlikely that we will use it in a careless or vainly repetitious manner. Although the breath prayer is frequently repeated, it is not some magical way to get results from God. Rather, it acts as a focus, and over time it becomes as much a part of us as our own breathing.

When I was a child, my grandmother taught me that anytime I heard a siren (fire, ambulance, police) I was to pray for the people involved in the emergency. The length of the prayer was not stressed, only the need to respond in spirit to those in trouble. As an adult I have continued the practice of praying whenever I hear a siren, and many people have shared with me that they do the same. Because I have repeated this behavior for so long, it—like the breath prayer—has become second nature to me.

*Does asking for a physical healing make a suitable breath prayer?*

Sometimes people who are ill respond to the question "What do you want?" by saying, "I want to be healed." Then I always ask, "If you were healed right now, how would you feel?"

"I'd feel peaceful," is a likely answer.

I then suggest a prayer based on that statement. Such a prayer might be, "Let me feel your peace, O God." This does not deny the reality of healing, but moves the focus beyond physical healing to the peace God offers, no matter what occurs.

*Do people ever find two breath prayers rise within them?*

Yes, people do sometimes find that two breath prayers emerge. When this happens, I suggest that they write both prayers down and ask themselves which is more personal. Which is moving more deeply into their being? Ted had discovered his prayer on a retreat, and after using that one prayer for several years, called to tell me that two prayers were emerging: "Let me feel your touch, O God" (his original breath prayer) and "Lead me in your way, O God." He shared that while working in a soup kitchen once a week he really felt touched by God when he handed lunch to the people who came through the line. For Ted it was time to let go of one prayer and move into the new one. In another circumstance it could be that the person felt touched by God and, finding that a little scary, wanted to hurry up and "get on the way." In that case I would suggest the person stay with the original prayer awhile longer.

People might also have two prayers emerge when they are facing a decision or going through a trauma or short-term crisis. Over time, though, one prayer generally emerges and is used exclusively.

*Will my breath prayer ever change?*

Yes, your breath prayer may change. During an intensive time of growth, it is not uncommon for someone's prayer to change several times. On a week-long retreat, for example, some people may change their prayer one or two times as they recognize deeper levels of need and the yearning God has for them.

For the most part, however, people tend to go through the discovery process and then keep that same breath prayer for a considerable time. If our prayer changes, it typically happens when we arrive at an insight or experience a significant life event such as marriage, death of a loved one, birth of a child, divorce, a job change, or resolution of a problem. During a time of transition we might use two prayers interchangeably. The emergence of a new prayer often occurs without our giving it any thought. One day we realize that we are saying a different prayer, a prayer that expresses our needs at a particular time in our life.

Some people use a prayer for two or three years and then quickly change to two or three prayers in the course of the next year. More often than not, however, people stay with the same prayer for long periods of time—some for as long as ten and fifteen years. The important thing to remember is that each person's experience with the breath prayer is unique, and there is no norm.

*One should refrain from changing the words of the prayer too often lest this frequent chopping and changing [of attention from one thing to another] should accustom the mind not to concentrate on one thing but to deviate from it and so remain for ever not firmly planted in itself; and thus it will bear no fruit, like a tree which is many times transplanted from place to place.*

✳

Callistus,
a fourteenth century spiritual teacher
From *Writings from the Philokalia on Prayer of the Heart*

*I have given up all my non-obligatory devotions and prayers and concentrate on being always in His holy presence; I keep myself in His presence by simple attentiveness and a loving gaze upon God which I can call the actual presence of God or to put it more clearly, an habitual, silent and secret conversation of the soul with God. . . .*

*As for time formally set aside for prayer, it is only a continuation of this same exercise. Sometimes I think of myself as a block of stone before a sculptor, ready to be sculpted into a statue, presenting myself thus to God and I beg Him to form His perfect image in my soul and make me entirely like Himself.*

From a letter of Brother Lawrence,
a seventeenth-century lay Carmelite
From *The Practice of the Presence of God*

# Learning to Pray Unceasingly

Learning to pray unceasingly is like acquiring any other good habit: it takes practice. Continuing to practice until a habit becomes second nature requires discipline. For example, when learning to knit, every stitch is painstakingly done, and we must check constantly to see if we are getting it right. But once we have mastered the skill, we can knit while carrying on a conversation or watching TV, seldom having to focus on the knitting.

Physical workouts such as jogging or aerobics also become second nature through practice. When we first commit to a regimen of exercise, the discipline is tedious. At times we wonder why we began. But there comes a point when we no longer have to give the activity our constant attention. We get to a place where we flow with the movement; our body moves with the rhythm. The inner person and the outer person are in harmony.

Likewise if prayer is to become part of our being, it requires attentiveness and discipline. Begin using your breath prayer as often as possible, saying it everywhere and under all circumstances. Say the prayer slowly, focusing on each word. The purpose is not to match the prayer to the sometimes hectic pace of your life, but to bring your entire being into harmony with a calm inner self.

A good time to practice your prayer is while walking. Use half your prayer on one step and half on the other. Or walk slowly and say the whole prayer on each step. If you do some form of exercise or body movement, say the prayer in rhythm with your movement. Many people use their breath prayer while running, jogging, or swimming. At first say your prayer slowly, almost gently; after a time your breath and your prayer will take on a rhythm of their own.

When you are alone, you may want to say your prayer out loud. Some people sing or chant their prayer. Changing the emphasis on the words often helps the prayer become more and more your own. Many people tell me they find this very helpful because they explore and discover various aspects and nuances of the prayer. For example:

> *O God,* let me feel your love.
> O God, *let* me feel your love.
> O God, let *me* feel your love.
> O God, let me *feel* your love.

As you use the prayer more and more, it develops within you through a process that involves the following stages:

### First Stage

In the first—or oral stage—we are aware of saying the prayer and it "resides," so to speak, in the throat and mouth. This stage is an essential part of our growth with the prayer and not vain repetition as discussed in Chapter 6. To call upon God is not vainly repetitious but a constant response to God's great love for us.

Learning a new way to pray requires attention and discipline. In this first stage you may find it helpful to have reminders that stimulate you to remember your commitment to the prayer.

• Many people write their prayers on note cards or labels and put them in places where they will see them often: the bathroom mirror, the refrigerator door, by the phone, on the dashboard. A lawyer put a small self-adhesive sticker-dot on his watch, and every time he checked the time he was reminded to say his prayer.

• A teacher prays every time the bell rings at school or the phone rings at home.

• A bank teller prays every time someone comes to his window.

• A woman whose favorite color is yellow prays whenever she sees something yellow.

• A dentist initially used her prayer each time she washed her hands at the office. Now she remembers her prayer every time she washes her hands.

• A sales rep who spends a lot of hours in his car uses his breath prayer whenever he glances in the rearview mirror.

• A doctor says the prayer each time she enters a hospital room.

Reminders to say our prayer are as personal as the prayer itself. As the prayer becomes more and more a part of us, the need to be reminded lessens.

I use my prayer in a variety of situations. If I am in traffic that tempts me to lay on the horn, I say my prayer instead. It has a calming influence and reminds me to respond lovingly to others. I have a dot on the frame of my computer screen, and it reminds me to be more attentive to God in the midst of my work. Sometimes I focus on the prayer for ten or fifteen seconds and feel myself move more consciously into the presence of God.

## Second Stage

You will be growing into this stage when the prayer moves into your mind. One day you will find yourself saying the prayer and be unaware of having said it. Or you will wake up in the morning and feel that you have been praying all night because the prayer is with you. At other times, too, you will find that the prayer is simply there, moving in and out of your consciousness. It might happen while you are walking or standing in line or waiting for an appointment. Then you will know that you are moving more and more into unceasing prayer.

The temptation at this stage is to sit back and enjoy the experience. After all, hasn't the prayer become so much a part of you that you no longer have to consciously focus on it? Although that may seem to be the case, it is still as important to pray consciously as it was in the first stage. The goal is to have your thoughts and actions become more and more integrated.

At this stage we—and perhaps the people around us—become aware of changes in our behavior. We no longer get so upset in traffic. We are more loving. We listen intently. We feel at peace and have the sense that we are growing closer to God. We enjoy silence more. We can be alone without feeling lonely. Difficult tasks go more smoothly. We become aware that our prayer is beginning to influence our entire life.

During this stage the prayer resides in our head, and has begun integrating our thoughts. One young man at this stage said, "A lot of thoughts that had been troubling me are now gone because I have something else on my mind." As we use the breath prayer, the work of the Spirit continues to transform us into God's image and likeness.

### Third Stage

In this stage the prayer moves into the heart. The shift comes about as we continue to pray with fervor and become more disciplined. It is as though the mind itself has moved into the heart and a union of the two takes place. When this occurs, our awareness of peace and love are increased; we think with love and make decisions based on that love. We find ourselves opening our hearts to others, recognizing both their suffering and their joy and becoming more conscious of how our prayer unites in spirit with them.

### Fourth Stage

In this last stage of the integration process, the prayer moves so totally into our lives that it moves throughout our body. So deep is the rhythm of the breath prayer that it unites with our breathing and is truly part of our being. After having used her prayer for four years, Cecelia describes how integrated the prayer can be:

> When I am faithful with my breath prayer and I awake at night there is a pulse, a rhythm. I am experiencing my body praying for me as I sleep. Through my breath prayer I have found a

way to have a constant attitude, a way of turning to God with my mind, heart, and soul—my
whole body. This way of praying has led me to
experience God's love in ways I never expected.
God *is* a God of glad surprises.

Because we are all different, the time it takes for each
stage varies. For most people, the passage from stage to
stage takes months, even years. So if you think your pro-
gress is slow, don't be discouraged. At whatever stage
you find yourself, there is something valuable to be
gained. Whether you are beginning and the prayer seems
to reside in the mouth, or whether it has begun to be a
part of your whole being, continued used of the prayer
will deepen your awareness of your life in God.

Begin praying your breath prayer. Say it at an even
pace over and over. At times you may feel this is a silly,
even childish thing to be doing, and that you cannot say
the prayer one more time. That is the point at which to
say it twenty times more. Discipline yourself to go on,
and the time will come when you are praying unceasingly.

> *The fruit*
> *and the purpose*
> *of prayer*
> *is*
> *to be oned with*
> *and like*
> *God*
> *in all things.*

Julian of Norwich
(1342–1416/1423)
English mystic
From *Meditations with Julian of Norwich*

*When the Spirit has come to reside in some-
one, that person cannot stop praying; for the
Spirit prays without ceasing in him. No matter if he is asleep or awake, prayer is going on
in his heart all the time. He may be eating or
drinking, he may be resting or working—the
incense of prayer will ascend spontaneously
from his heart. . . . His thoughts will be
prompted by God. The slightest stirring of his
heart is like a voice which sings in silence and
in secret to the Invisible.*

✳

Isaac the Syrian,
sixth-century monk, bishop, and writer
From *Teach Us to Pray*

# C H A P T E R    8

# *The Breath Prayer Brings Change*

Steven was a young husband, father, and dentist with a flourishing practice who was seeking a spiritual center in his life. "Can it really be true that God hears my breath prayer?" he asked. "Or am I praying just for me? It's hard for me to believe that it's possible to know—I mean *really* know—God. If only there were some magic words that would make this happen."

Having discovered his breath prayer, Steven was finding it difficult to get into the discipline of using it. This led him to question everything related to his spiritual life. He did not yet understand that to wonder in the depths of ourselves is the beginning of a great journey. Questioning is something we all go through on our way to a deeper spirituality.

Like Steven, we, too, may wish for something to instantly put us in union with God. This is understandable, given that we live in a society in which we want instant gratification and expect instant results. Even though we are conditioned to believe that change occurs quickly, it seldom does. Instead, God prepares the soil in which our spirituality takes root, and then tends us with loving care. But we also have a part to play. We need to make a conscious effort to continue to grow, and one of the ways to do this is through use of the breath prayer. Attentiveness to prayer increases our awareness of the presence of God in our lives. This awareness leads us to be more insightful about ourselves and our relationship with God. But instead of happening in a flash, change and growth come about gradually.

The change required of us calls to mind the scripture "Again I tell you, it is easier for a camel to go through the eye of a needle than for someone who is rich to enter the kingdom of God" (Matt. 19:24). Some scripture scholars believe that the eye of a needle in this passage refers to one of the narrow gates of Jerusalem. Before a camel could go through, the driver had to remove all that the camel carried. Only when the camel was unburdened could it pass through that gate into Jerusalem.

We all carry baggage that encumbers our lives—baggage that includes possessions, relationships, ambitions, hurtful feelings, memories of past failures. Some attachments are necessary and good, but a red flag goes up when we are compulsively attached to any of them. In one case a woman was so attached to her car that she asked to be buried in it; in another case, a son assaulted his parents because he felt smothered by their love. Even though these attachments are extreme, they motivate us to look at our own lives and see what changes are necessary to bring us into better balance. And unlike the camel that had to take its burden back after passing through the gate, we have the option of staying unburdened.

Robert's use of the breath prayer led him to an awareness that he needed to unburden his life. At age thirty-three, he was a pastor in a church that had just completed a building program on which he had spent so much time that he was out of touch with his prayer life. This is how he expressed himself in a journal entry:

I need to reorder some aspects of my life. I need to stop buying things and get out of debt. I need to start seeing Jesus in everyone. I need to care for my body and get going on some exercise. I need to bridle my anger. I'm becoming aware that it's like getting rid of a stubborn stain: each time I wash it, it gets lighter and lighter, but then I find another stain somewhere else.

Rose was a widow of means who could satisfy all of her material needs and most of her wants. In a journal entry, she told what happened after she settled into regular use of the breath prayer:

I was finding little things I could do without, and it made it so practical because they were things I'd been wanting to cut out for a long time, but the discipline of the breath prayer and my growing awareness of God's caring for me are making it easier.

At first we may be reluctant to unpack our camel, but when we do, we discover that we did not even want everything we were carrying. This can be likened to moving. The beginning stage of any move is seeing what possessions we can discard—things we won't need where we're going. Getting down to those things in life that are really important underlies the entire process of change. The more we recognize our compulsive attachments, the more we see ourselves as we really are.

Seeing ourselves as we are leads to a growth in humility. Humility has sometimes been considered self-deprecating—a matter of putting ourselves down—when, in fact, this is not the case at all. To be humble is to recognize the truth about who we are before God and others. This involves recognizing our strengths as well as our weaknesses.

For a long time, I was unable to accept a compliment. If someone said, "That's a beautiful shirt," I invariably responded by saying that it was old or that it was just something I picked up on sale. If someone told me my teaching was great, I laughed (a good defense, of course) and said, "Oh, I bet you say that to all your teachers." I was never able to say a simple thank you and leave it at that. But then an incident occurred that gave me a lesson in humility—a lesson from which I benefited greatly.

At the time I was in Cleveland, Ohio, and had given what I believed to be an especially good presentation one Saturday evening. Afterward a young woman who introduced herself as Mary came up to me. She had a warm smile, and in a forthright manner said, "Ron, that was the most beautiful talk I ever heard. You moved something within me."

I laughed self-consciously, and really did mean it when I said, "Oh, yes, the Spirit of God does wonders."

Instantly Mary's friendliness turned to anger. "That's the whole trouble with you Christians!" she yelled. "Can't you ever take responsibility for anything? You always think you're so special that you have to proclaim the Spirit is with you. Are you afraid we won't see it?"

Mary forced me to see that instead of being humble, I was unwittingly making myself special by *not* accepting her compliment. What she needed from me was a simple thank you; saying that would have been my ministry to her. But instead of focusing on her, I immediately turned the attention back on myself. The experience with Mary pointed up that when we walk in the Spirit there is no need to proclaim it in loud words. It is something we proclaim by the way we live our lives.

False humility prompted me to respond to Mary in a way that was less than honest. Honesty is perhaps the greatest gift we can bring to our relationships. And often being honest means saying no. I spent many years saying yes when I wanted to say no and then complaining about what I had agreed to. My work suffered and I realized that instead of being in control of situations, I was letting situations control me. Gradually I came to understand that I seldom said no because I didn't want to admit there were things I didn't want to do, or didn't do well. Also, saying yes was a subtle way to get people to notice me and love me.

Most of the people with whom I share agree that saying no is difficult. But doing so is critical if we are to have the time needed to replenish ourselves spiritually. Even Jesus said no to demands placed on him when he needed to go away by himself.

Tom, a husband and father of three teenagers, began using the breath prayer and realized that he had to say no to some of his activities in the community if he was going to restructure his life. In his journal he tells how using the breath prayer brought him to this realization:

Before, I was so busy doing all the good things that I had really forgotten to leave time to pray. I was using every second to plan my life and what I would do next. Now, using the breath prayer, I spend much more time being aware of living in God's presence, which I always was. I was just not as aware as I could be.

When we become aware of living in God's presence, we also develop the sense that *where we are is where we are supposed to be.* For many people this is a liberating idea. Given that we live in a society in which we are told we have to get through this and get through that in order to get on with something else, it is difficult to comprehend that in our life with God *there is no place to get to; there is only a life to live.*

Too often people feel that spiritual growth is a job that needs doing and that to earn God's love they have to work harder and harder. I believe this is faulty thinking on both counts: God's love is not something we have to earn, and in the spiritual life the premise that more is better is replaced by the idea that simpler is better. That is not to say we cannot lead involved and busy lives; but at the center of our being we need a single-minded focus on God. The breath prayer helps us maintain that focus and keeps us living in the present instead of looking back at the past or ahead to the future.

After using the breath prayer for a number of years, Jean, a mother of two small children who was involved in many causes, shared how she grew to value the here and now:

> My life relationships have become much smoother as a result of my efforts. I became more in tune with myself, my body, my work. I have become more loving and tolerant of people. I see them as having a beauty of their own. I

live only periodically in that loved space, and have not given myself completely to God's love, but more and more each day I feel a letting go. I am between two worlds—desiring not to go back and yet unable to jump into the future. I am striving perhaps too hard for that total change, but I know that where I am now is where I am supposed to be. God loves me in the here and now. That is my place to love.

As we move more and more into the presence of God, there is no way we can remain the same. God's loving action transforms us and we, in turn, become more loving toward those with whom we live and work and play. But for most of us, change comes slowly—so slowly sometimes that we wonder if it is happening at all. During those times be patient and continue praying. Change is occurring within you, and in due time, you will experience the graces of remaining faithful to your prayer.

*Imagine a circle with its centre and radii or rays going out from this centre. The further these radii are from the centre the more widely are they dispersed and separated from one another; and conversely, the closer they come to the centre, the closer they are to one another. Suppose now that this circle is the world, the very centre of the circle, God, and the lines (radii) going from the centre to the circumference or from the circumference to the centre are the paths of men's lives. Then here we see the same. In so far as the saints move inwards within the circle toward its centre, wishing to come near to God, then, in the degree of their penetration, they come closer both to God and to one another; moreover, inasmuch as they come nearer to God, they come nearer to one another, and inasmuch as they come nearer to one another, they come nearer to God.*

Abba Dorotheus,
a spiritual director in the beginning of the
seventh century. From a sermon delivered to
his students
From *Early Fathers from the Philokalia*

*Sooner or later, in varying degrees, the power and redeeming energy of God will be manifested through those who thus reach out in desire, first towards Him and then towards other souls. And we, living and growing personalities, are required to become ever more and more spiritualised, ever more and more persuasive, more and more deeply real; in order that we may fulfill this Divine purpose.*

*This is not mere pious fluff. This is a terribly practical job; the only way in which we can contribute to the bringing in of the Kingdom of God. Humanitarian politics will not do it. Theological restatement will not do it. Holiness will do it.*

✳

Evelyn Underhill (1875-1941)
From *Concerning the Inner Life*

# A Turning Point

Many people who use the breath prayer and become more aware of God's presence experience what has been called "the gift of tears." This is more than crying. The gift of tears is an experience of being overwhelmed by a sense of oneself in relationship to God. In this intimate and awesome state, we find ourselves crying and there seems to be no way to stop the flow of tears. Our awareness of how much we are loved by God just as we are, without judgment, fills us to overflowing with gratitude. Scripture tells us that on one occasion, a woman went to a house where Jesus had been invited for dinner, and while there, experienced the gift of tears:

> And a woman in the city, who was a sinner, having learned that he [Jesus] was eating in the Pharisee's house, brought an alabaster jar of ointment. She stood behind him at his feet, weeping, and began to bathe his feet with her tears and to dry them with her hair. Then she continued kissing his feet and anointing them with the ointment.
>
> Luke 7:37-38

Tears might also come when we see more clearly how we have denied our love and turned away from God. Such was the experience of the disciple Peter:

But Peter said, "Man, I do not know what you are talking about!" At that moment, while he was still speaking, the cock crowed. The Lord turned and looked at Peter. Then Peter remembered the word of the Lord, how he had said to him, "Before the cock crows today, you will deny me three times." And he went out and wept bitterly.

Luke 22:60-62

Most of the time the gift of tears is like a cloudburst; the floodgates open and we cry as if there is no stopping. In this entry from my own journal, I describe the experience I shared earlier about talking with one of my graduate school professors:

When you suggested we pray together and said, "As our savior Christ has taught us we are bold to say," I could feel a lump forming in my throat and I didn't know whether or not I'd be able to pray. I blurted, "Our Father" and then was overwhelmed with tears.

Martha, a grade school teacher who drove back and forth to work, made this journal entry about her gift of tears:

I don't know what was happening, but I was just sitting in the car at the intersection waiting for the light to change and saying the prayer. All of a sudden I started to cry. I was so aware of how much God loved me. It only lasted a moment, but it seemed like I'd broken through into a new place.

The gift of tears is a turning point in people's lives—a time of going deeper into the life of the Spirit. The apostle Paul talks about this in one of his letters:

> You were taught to put away your former way of life, your old self . . . and to be renewed in the spirit of your minds, and to clothe yourselves with the new self, created according to the likeness of God in true righteousness and holiness.
>
> Ephesians 4:22-24

In scripture and throughout our history as Christians, the gift of tears has marked spiritual turning points. Sometimes when we "lose control" and cry, we try to ignore what has happened or make light of it. But there is no denying what has taken place. James, a businessman in his early thirties, had just finished reading the above quote from Ephesians when he experienced the gift of tears. He described what happened in this journal entry:

> I then felt the beginning, the beginning of the new me, the beginning of the touch of the love of God. I felt appreciation, gratitude, and love. I then walked out into the rain, humble, and felt the rain and the cleansing comfort. There were small instances when my old Me came out and said, "This is foolish; this event is silly," but those feelings didn't stay very long because the old Me didn't have any lasting power.

Through the gift of tears, the power of living in the presence of God becomes more dynamic. We have a sense of mission or ministry or caring for others. We also have a renewed interest in loving and a more intense desire for prayer. It is as though we have been pushed from one dimension to another where we sense a new light and new possibilities for living.

It is not uncommon that after experiencing the gift of tears, our breath prayer changes. Edward was a seminary student whose prayer was "Jesus let me walk with you." One afternoon at a retreat on spirituality he asked to talk with me. The two of us went for a walk around a nearby lake, and Edward began to unravel his concerns about his family. Especially he talked about the hostility he felt toward certain family members. As we walked along the path, Edward stopped suddenly. He seemed transformed as he looked at me and said, "You know, *Jesus is walking with us right now.*"

"Yes, he is," I responded.

At that moment, Edward's eyes were opened and—like the apostle Paul—scales of darkness that had been holding back insights into his life fell away. The Spirit of truth was making Edward free. Pieces of his life and the mosaic of his relationship with God and his family came into focus. We continued our walk in prayer as Edward's tears flowed.

Later that evening a downcast Edward came to me. "I just can't say my prayer anymore," he said. "Asking Jesus to let me walk with him no longer fits." But even as Edward spoke, a knowing look came over his face. With awe in his voice, he said, "Maybe that's because I already have walked with Jesus. When you and I were going around the lake, I experienced walking with him!"

I suggested to Edward that the time had come for him to sit in silence and another prayer would be known to him. At this point in his life he would have another answer to God's question, "Edward, what do you want?"

Edward's acceptance of the gift of tears made him a good deal more conscious of God's presence in his life, and he was moved to serve others in greater love. Perhaps you, too, will experience the gift of tears on your journey to a deeper understanding of God's love. If so, regard the experience as a blessing and know that it is a sign of growth in the Spirit.

*Astonishing and stately is our soul—*
*the place where our Lord lives.*

*Therefore God wants us to respond*
*whenever we are touched,*
*rejoicing more in God's complete love*
*than sorrowing over*
*our frequent failings.*

Julian of Norwich (1342–1416/1423)
From *Meditations with Julian of Norwich*

*I urge you, then, pursue your course relent-
lessly. Attend to tomorrow and let yesterday
be. Never mind what you have gained so far.
Instead reach out to what lies ahead. If you do
this you will remain in the truth. For now, if
you wish to keep growing you must nourish in
your heart the lively longing for God. Though
this loving desire is certainly God's gift, it is
up to you to nurture it. . . . Press on then. I
want to see how you fare. Our Lord is always
ready. He awaits only your co-operation.*

✳

From one of the letters of an unknown
spiritual director of the fourteenth century
From *The Cloud of Unknowing*

# The Breath Prayer Becomes
# Part of Life

Some beautiful new houses were built at the end of the street where we once lived. But as those houses stood in the middle of their lots surrounded only by dirt, they didn't fit in with the setting. Although the houses were complete in themselves, they stood apart from one another, giving the neighborhood a disjointed look. Then one morning a truck from the local nursery arrived and landscapers went to work. Within days they had laid all the sod and planted shrubbery. What a change! Now greenery joined the new houses with the others on the block, and suddenly the neighborhood looked unified.

The breath prayer serves much the same purpose as the greenery around the houses in that it unites and unifies all our ways of praying. No single form of prayer is weakened, changed, or neglected. Instead, each is enhanced because the breath prayer brings a new depth and dimension to familiar ways of praying.

As we practice praying unceasingly, we become more and more conscious of living in God's presence. We have a better grasp of what it is to be a child of God, as expressed in this scripture:

> For all who are led by the Spirit of God are
> children of God. For you did not receive a spirit

of slavery to fall back into fear, but you have received a spirit of adoption. When we cry, "Abba! Father!" it is that very Spirit bearing witness with our spirit that we are children of God, and if children, then heirs, heirs of God and joint heirs with Christ—if, in fact, we suffer with him so that we may also be glorified with him.

Romans 8:14-17

As children of God, we increasingly walk in the light. Therefore we have less to fear because of scripture's assurance that even in the dark, we have the light that is Jesus to follow:

What has come into being in him was life, and the life was the light of all people. The light shines in the darkness, and the darkness did not overcome it.

John 1:3-5

Unceasing prayer keeps us mindful that we are children of God, and as such walk in a light that will see us through any difficulty. But making prayer as much a part of our lives as breathing requires discipline. Friends with whom I have shared in spiritual direction kid me because of the many times they have heard me say, "Discipline is the key."

Sometimes prayer comes with ease. It is not hard to pray when we feel moved by the Spirit or when we find ourselves in desperate situations. Neither is it hard to pray when we are in a good mood and things are going well or when we are with people who pray as we do. But remember, we are called to do more than pray when prayer comes easily; we are called to become prayerful people—to be people who pray always in the Spirit, in the breath of God. The more aware we are of our call to be people of prayer, the greater our awareness that our breath and the breath of God are becoming one.

The only way to find out what effect placing yourself in God's presence will have on your life is to try it. When you feel an urge to make an unkind remark, silently say your breath prayer. When you feel a need to top someone's story, say the prayer. When you find yourself getting angry, say the prayer. Pray when waiting at a stoplight or for an appointment. Pray while hugging the children or teaching a class. Center on your breath prayer while you do the dishes or paint the house. Turn off the radio when you drive and say your breath prayer. Instead of watching TV after dinner, go for a walk and pray. Over time you will discover that by praying more and more unceasingly you feel an overflow of love—a love that goes out to others. This becomes a deep form of intercessory prayer.

Many of us spend most of our time with others. Because we are so seldom alone, we are like a pendulum stuck to one side, out of balance. As the breath prayer becomes more a part of you, don't be surprised if you want to spend additional time alone or feel a need for a few minutes of silence each day. To rebalance your schedule, enter silence and pray. For some people this is almost a foreign experience; that is how accustomed we have become to relentless activity.

As you continue using your breath prayer, your pace tends to slow and you feel a greater integration of mind, body, and spirit. You are more in tune with your work.

You begin freeing yourself from compulsive attachments, whether they be to behaviors, objects, or people. You become more honest about your abilities and your life. You are more patient, and you likely will find your horizons widening or shifting.

We all have a horizon upon which we base our actions. It is the familiar base from which we operate. As long as that horizon, or base, is there—and we see it—we can get our bearings and go on with life. After important life events such as a marriage, a death, a birth, the loss of a job, a graduation, a birthday marking a new decade, or a significant insight, we need to reestablish our horizon.

As we use the breath prayer, old horizons widen or shift and new possibilities appear. Having someone with whom to share our spiritual growth helps us see and explore the possibilities. We grow not as individuals alone but as individuals within a community. Even though we may feel we are praying alone, our prayer unites us with all who pray and are attentive to God's presence. The more attentive we are to God, the more attentive and caring we become to others as well. Prayer brings us into a fullness with God wherein we are motivated to work for social justice and take a stand against oppression in its various forms.

Ken was an insurance salesman who had been using his prayer for about two years when he said to me, "I'm feeling that it's not right for me to just pray daily. I've got to do something." What Ken did was work with the homeless in his community. He later told me that he found great value and a deep sense of touching God through his work in an overnight shelter. "I use my breath prayer as I say goodnight to the people," he said. "It reminds me that I'm in God's presence."

Any teacher in the area of spirituality, or friend knowledgeable about the subject, will assure you that your present horizon is what it should be for where you are right now. At the same time that teacher or friend will encourage you to move on. If you do not have someone with whom to share, look for such a person. To have something in common to talk over, give that person a copy of this book. Consider the counselors, ministers, or leaders you know, and see if you are drawn to one of them. Perhaps you could join or start a prayer study group. Seek to develop relationships in which you can communicate your feelings about the spiritual journey you are on.

The breath prayer provides us with common ground. Even though we each have our own prayer, we know that others who have a prayer are praying unceasingly. When I go into a group and recognize someone who I know uses a breath prayer, it is a warming experience.

In a neighborhood where we once lived, there was a post office notorious for its long lines at the lunch hour. (If I overuse the idea of praying while in line, it is because of my numerous experiences of doing so at this post office!) As I waited one day, I glanced at another line and noticed Barbara, a young woman who had attended one of my classes on the breath prayer. Our eyes met, and with a smile she said, "I know what you're doing, and I bet you know what I'm doing." We both laughed and continued waiting in line, in prayer.

The breath prayer enables us to be prayerful in the ordinary activities of life. By using the breath prayer as

much as possible at all times and in all places, we soon
realize what an enriching, vital part of our life it has become.

*True Friends*

*People will tell you that you do not*
*need friends on this journey,*
*that God is enough.*

*But to be with God's friends is a good way*
*to keep close to God in this life.*
*You will always draw great benefit from them.*

✳

Teresa of Avila (1515-1582)
From *Meditations with Teresa of Avila*

*Unceasing prayer consists in an unceasing invocation of the name of God. Whether talking, sitting, walking, making something, eating or occupied in some other way, one should at all times and in every place call upon the name of God, according to the command of Scripture: Pray without ceasing.*

*We must pray with the heart; we must also pray with the mouth, when we are alone. But if we are in the market, or in the company of others, we should not pray with the lips, but only with the mind.*

Kallistos,
a Byzantine spiritual writer,
fourteenth-fifteenth century
From *On the Prayer of Jesus: From the Ascetic Essays of Bishop Ignatius Brianchaninov*

# A Special Time and Place for Prayer

In addition to praying while doing whatever it is we are doing, we may also feel a need for a special time and place for prayer. *The length of time we take to be in prayer is not as important as the fact that we take the time.* What I suggest during this time is called "sitting prayer," because that is exactly what we do—we sit into a more intense time of being aware of the presence of God.

If you have never sat in prayer, start modestly—with five minutes, perhaps. If you are accustomed to sitting in silence, try ten. The idea is not to let yourself be ruled by a specified time, but to tailor the time to you and your spiritual needs. When we are excited about starting something new, it is tempting to set a lengthy time. But it is better to do five minutes regularly than twenty minutes today, five tomorrow, and ten the day after.

The key to success in sitting prayer is discipline. Some days you will look forward to the sitting-prayer time, and on others will wonder why you cannot sit still. In this sense, prayer is like training for the race that the apostle Paul speaks about:

> Do you not know that in a race the runners
> all compete, but only one receives the prize?
> Run in such a way that you may win it. Athletes

exercise self-control in all things; they do it to receive a perishable wreath, but we an imperish-
able one.

1 Corinthians 9:24-25

You will need a schedule and the inner discipline to
adhere to it. Here is where sharing with a friend or a
group can be a great help. Your sitting prayer needs to be
done in a place where you feel "at home" in prayer. This
might simply be a corner of a room where you have a
picture, a Bible, a candle, or something else that makes
the space special to you. If you are fortunate enough to
have an unused room, or one that is seldom used, make
that your place of prayer. For seating, it is preferable to
use a straight-back chair or to sit on the floor on a cush-
ion.

People intent on sitting in prayer become creative
about finding space. One woman cleaned out a closet and
then put her Bible and a favorite picture on the shelves.
When it is time for her sitting prayer, she opens the closet
door, moves a chair in front of the closet, and has her
special place.

A professional man does his sitting prayer when he
arrives at his office. He opens his closet door and sits
quietly in front of an icon of Jesus he has hung on the inside of the door.

Many people create their special place at a dining
room table. Each time they sit down to pray, they open
their Bible and light a candle.

Ritual is important, and I suggest that it be part of
your time spent in prayer. When getting ready to do
anything special, we usually go through a ritual: we get

dressed up for a night out, we have birthday and anniversary rituals, we even make special preparations before sitting down to watch a ball game or a long movie on TV. The following ritual helps us become more aware that our sitting prayer is a special time spent in God's presence.

### One

Wash your hands. The hand-washing serves as a reminder of a passage through water, which in scripture is seen as a transition into a new way of life or ministry to others. We see this in both the Hebrew and Christian scriptures:

> I will take you from the nations, and gather you from all the countries, and bring you into your own land. I will sprinkle clean water upon you, and you shall be clean from all your uncleannesses, and from all your idols I will cleanse you.
>
> Ezekiel 36:24-25

> And when Jesus had been baptized, just as he came up from the water, suddenly the heavens were opened to him and he saw the Spirit of God descending like a dove and alighting on him. And a voice from heaven said, "This is my Son, the Beloved, with whom I am well pleased."
>
> Matthew 3:16-17

## Two

Set a timer for the length of time you plan to be in prayer. (This makes it unnecessary for you to look at a watch or clock.) There will be days when five minutes will seem like one minute. Other days you will be certain you have prayed for half an hour, when in fact it has been only four minutes! A timer allows you to peacefully focus on prayer in the knowledge that when the time is up, a bell or buzzer will let you know.

## Three

Read a verse from scripture as a reminder that we are fed from the constancy of God's word. Read only a line or a verse. I recommend the Psalms or John's Gospel because a meaningful line or verse can readily be found there. The intent is not to ponder the scripture but to place ourselves more intently in the presence of God.

## Four

Sit in prayer. Slowly and rhythmically repeat your breath prayer. If random thoughts enter your mind, be assured that this is natural. As you become aware of the thoughts, calmly bring your focus back to the breath prayer. Writers in the early centuries of the church talk about the prayer bringing calm attentiveness. In our stillness we can be attentive.

Some people find it helpful to begin their sitting time by saying the breath prayer aloud, then saying it ever more softly until they become more and more silent within themselves. Remember that the nuance of the prayer can change, depending upon the words we emphasize: *God*, let me feel your peace. God, *let* me feel your peace. . . . Changing the emphasis of the words can help keep us attentive.

Once you have created a place to sit in prayer, decide on a time. Then commit yourself to sit in prayer daily. If your schedule varies, try to sit at least three or four days each week. The morning is best for most people only because the discipline is then taken care of and does not get pushed aside by other matters. One caution about praying in the morning, however, is that we may get caught up in what I call the "gas station mentality" of spirituality. I think especially of Bill, whose job required that he fly around the country. "My life just seems like I'm going eighty [miles per hour] all the time," he said. "If I don't get some prayer time in the morning, I get to the end of the day and it's as if I haven't thought of God at all. I've got to gas up in the morning so I can make it through the day."

Prayer is not something we do just to gas up. It is a way of life. Having a special place and time for prayer is good and spiritually rewarding, but our prayer for the day does not begin and end there. The important thing is that we are attentive to being in God's presence throughout the day, and the breath prayer enables us to do that.

*You must never regard any spiritual work as firmly established, and this is especially true of prayer; but always pray as if beginning for the first time. When we do a thing for the first time, we come to it fresh and with a new-born enthusiasm. If, when starting to pray, you always approach it as though you had never yet prayed properly, and only now for the first time wished to do so, you will always pray with a fresh and lively zeal. And all will go well.*

※

Theophan the Recluse,
nineteenth-century monk, bishop,
and spiritual director.
From *The Art of Prayer: An Orthodox Anthology*

*In this fashion we learn the*
*power*
*and the strength*
*of silence.*

*We learn to go into the world*
*as still as a mouse*
*in the depths of our heart.*

✳

Mechtild of Magdeburg
(c. 1209–c.1283)
From *Meditations with Mechtild*
*of Magdeburg*

# A Journal for Reflection

One of the best ways to reflect on your prayer is to keep a journal. After each time of sitting prayer, take three to five minutes to write in a notebook what you have experienced. *This is not meant to be a tedious task.* Simply write the date, the time of day, and at least two sentences about what happened during your prayer. You might note the thoughts you had, experiences you recalled, emotions you felt, or physical reactions. Journal entries reveal changes in the mind and heart much the way a family photo album shows physical changes.

Journals can be any size or kind. Some people prefer a size that will fit in the pocket. Others like to use notebook paper so the pages can be kept in a binder. Still others—myself included—do their journaling on a computer.

The following journal entries reveal the kinds of things people write. The entries were made during the first weeks of using the breath prayer. Rebecca, a retired government employee, did her journaling on the veranda of her Florida home:

> This journal kept getting in my way. Will I remember what to write down? All the outside sounds kept coming in—do the birds always chirp so loudly in the A.M.? Does the dog always breathe so heavily? A few really quiet seconds of

a peaceful feeling. And wonder of wonders, was ten minutes really so short?

A mother of two teenage daughters and very involved in church work, Mary Ellen reveals how her prayer time created an oasis of calm in a busy life:

> I am very quiet. Even to write seems an effort. I write slowly. Fifteen minutes seemed to have passed pleasantly and quickly. I was reluctant to stop. After perhaps five minutes I became very still, began to pray silently instead of out loud. My mind kept up an observing commentary, but the stillness surrounded all. The phone rang, and I knew I would not rise from my prayer to answer it.

Peter was a retired business executive whose mind was always so busy that it was difficult for him to become still:

> Felt very calm and peaceful. Found that my mind was wandering or blank, so I went back to the prayer. Felt calmer and more relaxed. My mind did not seem to wander as much.

An anesthesiologist and single father with teenage children, Jack reveals how through prayer he began to find his spiritual center:

> I became aware as I sat in prayer that I've known for some time that the power moving me in the direction I have been going the past four or more years was more powerful than I am.

The Spirit that is moving me will not let me stop. The pages will continue to be turned, and the traveler will go on by whatever mode of transportation.

Stephanie was a single woman in her late twenties with stylish clothes, a nice car, and everything going her way:

> Saying "Jesus, let me hear your voice." What am I asking? Am I ready to hear him? Ready to do whatever he asks of me? This is rather frightening. I know myself so well—will it be something I can't give up? I am weighing the questions.

The key to keeping a journal of your sitting prayer time is keeping it simple. The surest way to do this is to limit your writing time. If you are already keeping a journal, incorporate your sitting-prayer reflections in it, but key them in some way so they are easy to find when you want to refer to them in the future.

Drawing, sketching, painting, and collage-making are also ways of journaling. Visual journaling, in which people sketch instead of write, is gaining in popularity. It is not necessary to be skilled in art to do visual journaling.

At a retreat I was giving, Laura confided that she was having difficulty clarifying the issues she faced. She tried writing in her journal, but didn't find that to be very satisfactory. "Have you ever drawn anything—done any sketching?" I asked.

Laura said she enjoyed sketching and I suggested she keep a visual journal during her retreat. After each of her meditations, she drew a picture that described her experience. At the beginning of the retreat one of her drawings was of a big circle squished sideways. "I just felt like everything was closing in on me," she explained. At the end of the week, Laura showed me her sketch of the sun rising over a mountain scene. "I feel like the sun is just coming up in my life," she said.

> *The fullness of joy*
> *is*
> *to behold*
> *God*
> *in*
> *everything.*

※

Julian of Norwich
(1342–1416/1423)
English mystic
From *Meditations with
Julian of Norwich*

*How dear to me is your dwelling, O Lord of hosts!*
*My soul has a desire and longing for the courts of the*
*Lord;*
*my heart and my flesh rejoice in the living God.*

*The sparrow has found her a house*
*and the swallow a nest where she may lay her young;*
*by the side of your altars, O Lord of hosts,*
*my King and my God.*

*Happy are they who dwell in your house!*
*they will always be praising you.*

*Happy are the people whose strength is in you!*
*whose hearts are set on the pilgrims' way.*

✳

Psalm 84:1-4
*Book of Common Prayer, 1979*

# What Can You Hope to Experience?

I asked some people who have used the breath prayer over a period of time if they would share their experiences. They agreed in the hope that through their sharing, others would be encouraged to discover their breath prayer and find a new closeness with God.

Mary is a psychotherapist with grown children who has been using her breath prayer for thirteen years. She says that although there have been on and off times of being faithful to the prayer, she lives most of her daily life being attentive to God's presence. She still loves to dance when she prays, just as she did when she made this journal entry years ago:

> I've been using the breath prayer for a little longer than a year now, and I think the most important thing I've come to see is how closely my body is connected to my prayer. When I first began to use the prayer, I was tense and full of aches and pains when I did the sitting. Just sitting still was hard for me. I was always running. But I am continuing to slow down, to feel better and to be more aware of how important it is for me to be aware that my body is a gift from God.

Shawn, a psychologist who deals mainly with patients in crisis situations, tells how he uses his prayer in his work:

> I am a counselor, and after using the breath prayer for over two years, I find that I am able to use it in my practice more and more. I look at my clients and pray for them. I find I am more insightful and rely more on the promptings within me in my work. I know I am more loving.

Marie is an actress in community theater whose journal entry reveals her poetic side:

> I was forged in the fiery furnace, melted down in the flames of pain and lost in agony and fear and knowledge of my nothingness till all that was left was a spark, a tiny cinder. God breathed life on that spark till it became an eternal flame and I was born.

John sought spiritual direction during a mid-life crisis and made this entry:

> One great truth that has overwhelmed me is that while we can approach God as a loving Father, he is still sovereign over all. It is with awe and trembling that we receive this privilege. It was not cheap grace but a profound awareness of a level of existence more profound and powerful and bold than one could in human thought imagine.

Richard is a young pastor just starting his ministry in a large suburban parish:

> Leading the congregation in worship has changed for me since I have been using the breath prayer. I find myself praying during the silent periods. I find that I am more centered and at peace when I celebrate the worship.

When Theresa reached her mid-twenties, she began dealing with issues related to being rejected as a child:

> There has been much pain in seeing myself as I really was, but there has also been much joy. I feel most that I wish I had more people to share this great joy with.

Sam is an engineer, who in his middle years, was searching for meaning in his life:

> My life with God has been transformed. Praying unceasingly has led me into a state I never thought possible. To be in the presence of God and to be aware of that is a great gift. Praise be to God.

Alex, a clergyman in his late thirties, has been using the breath prayer over a period of years and shared his experiences with it in a newsletter to his congregation:

> "How would you respond if Jesus were to walk into the room and say, 'Alex, what do you want?' " That question was put to me ten years ago by Ron DelBene. . . .

The word "joy" immediately came to my mind. So I prayed, "Father, let me feel your joy." I taped this prayer inside my desk drawer. I wrote it in my calendar. I found ways to remind myself to pray this prayer many times each day. It became a "breath prayer" that I prayed for eight months.

Over time, the prayer was answered. It was time for a new prayer focus. While showering one morning at a weekend retreat . . . I prayed, "Father, radiate your love through me." The new prayer had a dual focus: to receive God's love through and through, and to be a vessel for sharing God's love. I prayed this prayer from October 1981 until May 1991.

In May, I was at a camp for a five-day session on spiritual formation. After a lecture we were asked to spend an hour reflecting on John 15. I sat in the chapel looking at a picture of Jesus. The word "abide" from John 15 converged with the large, inviting hand of Jesus in the picture to prompt another breath prayer: "Jesus, abide in me." For five months, this was my prayer. A breath prayer often leads one to other prayer concerns. A breath prayer can also lead one to another breath prayer. So, after five months, I began to note in my journal a shift in the prayer. Now, I'm praying, "Jesus, keep me simple."

Prayer, like compound interest for an investor, is cumulative. Simple people have joy. Love radiates through simple people. The Spirit of Christ abides in simple Christians.

This particular prayer may be the focus of my praying for a few months, or ten years, or eternity. I'll always remember that it was born in anticipation of Advent. "Jesus, keep me simple," is my way of preparing for Christmas this year.

Each of these breath prayers has been a gift from God. It's not just something my brain has generated. I receive these prayers as a gift to offer back to God in gratitude for the purpose of my transformation.

Just as each of us is unique, so too is our prayer life. No two people will experience the breath prayer in exactly the same way. What we all have in common, however, is the same God—the God who moves within and among us and unites us in the life of the Spirit. Through use of the breath prayer we grow in the Spirit and become more and more conscious of God's everlasting love and presence in our lives.

Often, though, we feel unworthy of God's love. And in a certain sense we are. After all, who are you and who am I? Among so many, we are as tiny grains of sand upon the beach. Yet we have each been called, and called right where we are—weak, not yet perfect, sometimes seeing ourselves as unlovable. But that is the great mystery of God who has chosen to love us where we are, as we are.

I invite you to join the growing number of people committed to unceasing prayer. Discover your breath prayer and practice it until it is so much a part of you that it comes as naturally as breathing. Do so and you will come to experience the breadth and depth of God's love in exciting and unexpected ways.

*The principal thing is to stand with the
mind in the heart before God, and to go
on standing before Him unceasingly day
and night, until the end of life.*

✳

Theophan the Recluse,
nineteenth-century monk, bishop, and
spiritual director
From *The Art of Prayer: An Orthodox Anthology*

*When are we like God?*
*I will tell you.*
*In so far as we love compassion*
*and practice it steadfastly,*
*to that extent*
*do we resemble the heavenly*
*Creator*
*who practices these things*
*ceaselessly in us.*

﹡

Mechtild of Magdeburg
(c. 1209–c. 1283)
From *Meditations with Mechtild of*
*Magdeburg*

# ACKNOWLEDGMENTS

*The publisher gratefully acknowledges permission to reprint the following copyrighted material:*

Excerpts from *The Art of Prayer*, compiled by Igumen Chariton of Valamo, translated by E. Kadloubovsky and E. M. Palmer. Copyright © 1966 by Elizabeth M. Palmer. Used by permission of Faber & Faber, Ltd.

Excerpt from *The Cloud of Unknowing*, edited by William Johnston, 1973. Used by permission of Doubleday, a division of Bantam, Doubleday, Dell Publishing Group, Inc.

Excerpt from *Concerning the Inner Life* by Evelyn Underhill. Copyright © 1926 by E. P. Dutton. Used by permission of the publisher, Dutton, an imprint of New American Library, a division of Penguin Books USA, Inc. and Methuen London, Ltd.

Excerpt from *Early Fathers from the Philokalia*, translated by E. Kadloubovsky and G. E. H. Palmer, 1981, © 1954. Used by permission of Faber & Faber, Ltd.

Excerpts from *Meditations with Julian of Norwich* by Brendan Doyle, Copyright 1983, Bear & Co. Reprinted with permission of Bear & Co., Inc., P.O. Box 2860, Santa Fe, NM 87504.

Excerpts from *Meditations with Mechtild of Magdeburg* by Sue Woodruff, Copyright 1982, Bear & Co. Reprinted with permission of Bear & Co., Inc., P.O. Box 2860, Santa Fe, NM 87504.

# A B O U T   T H E   A U T H O R S

The Rev. Ron DelBene holds a master's degree in theology and has done additional post-graduate work in education, psychology, and counseling. He has been assistant professor of theology, director of a campus ministry center, National Consultant in Religion for an education division of CBS, and Executive for Program and rector in parish ministry. He has worked with Cursillo, Walk to Emmaus, and Kairos, as well as with various denominational judicatories in retreat and spiritual formation work.

An Episcopal priest, Ron leads retreats, conferences, and training events across the country in spirituality and pastoral care. He has been doing spiritual direction since 1965. Ron is active in ministry with the sick and the dying and involved in working for peace and justice. With his wife, Eleanor, he directs The Hermitage, a place for people to enter into solitude and prayer under their direction.

Ron and Eleanor live in Trussville, Alabama, and have two grown children, Paul and Anne.

Mary and Herb Montgomery are full-time writers who have created numerous books and educational projects to help both children and adults grow in faith. The Montgomerys live in Minneapolis.